SAMMY WILLOS

CONTROL YOUR EMOTIONS

The Ultimate Guide on How to Achieve Emotional Balance, Learn the Useful Tips and Effective Methods on How to Master Control of Your Emotions for Life Success

Descrierea CIP a Bibliotecii Naționale a României
SAMMY WILLOS
  CONTROL YOUR EMOTIONS. The Ultimate Guide on How to Achieve Emotional Balance, Learn the Useful Tips and Effective Methods on How to Master Control of Your Emotions for Life Success / Sammy Willos – Bucharest: Editura My Ebook, 2020
  ISBN

SAMMY WILLOS

CONTROL YOUR EMOTIONS

**The Ultimate Guide on How to Achieve Emotional Balance,
Learn the Useful Tips and Effective Methods on How to
Master Control of Your Emotions for Life Success**

My Ebook Publishing House
Bucharest, 2020

TABLE OF CONTENTS

FOREWORD

Do you consider yourself as an emotional person? Do your emotions often make the best of you, controlling your life to the point that you no longer have any idea where you are actually going? Are your emotions the very reason why you find it difficult to deal with the different situations that happen day in and day out?

Most people today often find themselves tangled in different emotions and combine this with all the stresses of today's life, it is only understandable when some end up consumed by their emotions.

But if you want to be truly successful, one of the important things that you need to learn is emotional equilibrium or the perfect balance betweenyour emotions.

In this book, you can expect to learn about the different and most vital information that you need to know about your emotions in general and how you can fully control them and how to balance them properly for you to achieve your much coveted success.

Emotional Equilibrium

Gain Control Of Your Emotions For Life Success

CHAPTER 1

EMOTION BASICS

Synopsis

Emotions are already a part of human nature. But how much do you really know about emotions? What are emotions? What are their elements? What are the most common types of emotions? This chapter is where you will learn the basics of emotions for you to get started.

Emotions seem to be like a king that rules your day to day life. The decisions that you make are based on whether you are happy, sad, bored, frustrated or angry. Your hobbies and activities are chosen based on the kind of emotions that they incite. But what exactly are emotions?

By definition, emotions are complex psychological states involving three unique components: subjective experience, physiological response and expressive or behavioral response.

A Glimpse into the World of Emotions

Aside from trying to understand what exactly emotions are, the researchers also tried identifying and classifying the various types of emotions. Paul Eckman, a psychologist, suggested in 1972 that there are actually 6 basic emotions that can be considered universal in the entire human cultures, namely anger, fear, disgust, surprise, sadness, and happiness. But in 1999, he further expanded the list, including some other basic emotions such as excitement, embarrassment, contempt, pride, shame, amusement and satisfaction.

In the 1980s, Robert Plutchik introduced the so-called wheel emotions, another kind of emotion classification system. In this model, it was demonstrated how various emotions can be mixed or combined together, in the same way that artists combine the primary colors in order to come up with secondary colors. He suggested that there are actually eight primary emotional dimensions, including fear versus anger, sadness versus happiness, disgust versus trust and anticipation versus surprise. These emotions can then be mixed in various ways. For instance, anticipation and happiness can be combined to create excitement.

But what are really the purposes of your emotions? What do they do for you? Certainly, these have an important effect on you but what are these all for?

Your Emotions are Your Motivation

Your emotions motivate you. Without them, you will never be able to do much, thus, you will not survive, which is applicable to the evolved form that you are now. Your body can feel motivations. Your muscles either relax or tense. Your blood vessels contract or dilate. When you feel emotional, you can also feel this physically. It means that your emotions can either make you comfortable or uncomfortable, sending signals for you to do something right away or just stay in your comfortable state.

Your Emotions are Your Social Signals

In general, people wear their hearts on their sleeves as their inner emotions are being displayed on their outer bodies. Your face in particular has about 90 muscles wherein 30 have the main purpose of signaling your emotions to others. These signals are very useful for they let other people decide how to behave toward you. When you look angry, those around you will never think of attacking you.

Your Emotions Serve as Internal Signals

For instance, internally, when you try to make a decision or understand something, you use your emotions to determine if your conclusion is a good idea. When you think of something that contradicts your values, your emotions are going to tell you that this is bad. When you think of something that can hurt you, your emotions are going to tell you that the idea is not good. By simply imagining what can happen, your emotions will be triggered, thus letting you come up with better decisions.

CHAPTER 2

EVALUATE YOUR EMOTIONS

Synopsis

There are times when you find it hard to identify what you really feel. You do not know if you are irritated or angry or something much worse than that. People's emotions can become too confusing at times and for this reason, it is a must that you learn to evaluate your emotions, which is exactly what will be discussed in this chapter.

Ways on Getting Your Emotions Evaluated

You feel messed up and instead of doing something to figure out the reason behind this, you just resort to telling yourself that life is really unfair and you are a terrible person. However, not being able to distinguish between your negative emotions and letting them lump together to form into a miserable mess can actually lead to great deals of emotional stress based on the latest study.

Experts state that those who find it difficult to distinguish one emotion from another usually have a sense of unpleasantness in general. If you cannot differentiate your emotions, you will find it harder to act in the appropriate way.

For you to get to the bottom of what you are truly feeling, there are several things that you can try to get your emotional knots completely untangled.

Give yourself some time out. Every day, try to allot some time for decompression. Take note that you have no capacity of reacting properly to a certain situation when you still carry the emotions of the earlier time in your day.

You can try training your emotional brain. Not all people have the ability of identifying their emotions that are more nuanced but you can at least try honing your skills by starting with what you can. Try identifying your emotions beyond what is unpleasant. Is it guilt? Anger? Or shame? Simply asking these questions can already help you in pinpointing your angst.

Write things down. When you find it hard to identify your various emotions, try to jot down your feelings. Patterns will start to form that can help you in differentiating one emotion to another.

Check your gut. Are you reacting to a physical sensation or to an emotion? When doubtful, rule out the physical causes of your feelings such as hunger and lack of sleep.

Take a stroll. You probably think that your busy day is over once you walk out the door but if you still have a racing pulse, chances are your emotional state is still controlled by your physiology. Taking a walk is the best choice when it comes to emotional regulation. This directs your attention inward, helping you to refocus.

Clean up your clutter. Having a clean and tidy space will be able to help you focusing your thoughts where they are required to be. Mental or physical clutter can both add to your overall sense of disarray. If you find it hard to focus, the mere act of cleaning and its result will be able to help in clearing your mind.

CHAPTER 3

UNDERSTAND WHERE YOUR EMOTIONS COME FROM

Synopsis

Do you know where your emotions are coming from? In the same way that you cannot understand why a certain person acts like that when you do not know his or her background, you will also not be able to comprehend your emotions when you do not know where they come from in the first place. By understanding where your emotions are coming, emotional balance can become more possible.

There are some people who assume that your emotions are stemming from your thoughts. But the truth is, this is completely wrong as there is a little bit more involved than your thoughts alone. Your emotions are not only about what you think about or how you put your attention to them. In contrast to some of the present self help philosophy, a person's emotions do not only come from his or her thoughts alone.

Discover the True Source of Your Emotions

Did you ever experience listening to a comedian who tells his tragic story while adding a sense of fun to it? Comedians have this skill of discussing their relationship breakups, the collapse of the economy or even war in such a way that makes you laugh about it. These people make you think of tragedies and laugh with true joyful emotions regarding them. Obviously, there is something more than the subject matter or thoughts to create emotions. In a way, something in your point of view can affect the emotions that you create.

On the other hand, in some other moments that you think about a breakup, an economic challenge or war, it is no longer funny. You quickly feel anger, sadness, despair and injustice. If you believe that it is only your thoughts or what you put your attention on is what creates emotions, then you have accepted a plain answer and give up on the real truth.

Among the truths that people overlook is that you are the one that creates your emotions. This is overlooked because there are instances when they say things like "That is frightening" or

"She is the reason for my happiness." These things sound as if other people or situations created your emotions, without a mention of yourself being the one responsible for a certain aspect of this process. Believing such thoughts or comments can make you overlook your role in creating your emotions.

Another thing that can affect your emotions is your point of view that you use when observing a thought. Comedians have the humorous perspective regarding tragic events that can make you laugh when you look at it from their viewpoint. Politicians discuss a similar situation using a viewpoint invoking a feeling or righteousness or patriotism. Meanwhile, the point of view of the victim looking at the similar situation will cause him or her to feel sad. The point of view you use for perceiving events or from where your thoughts come from can affect the emotions that you create.

It is not only what you are thinking about but more about the viewpoint you think about this from that leaves an impact. Depending on the viewpoint that you have, you can come up with different interpretations thus making you believe various assumptions. Beliefs are then formed when you believed in these assumptions and interpretations or these activate your existing beliefs which can also have an effect on the emotions that youmake as well as the level of their strength.

Your emotions are a powerful energy form or power and this comes from faith, a kind of personal power that can turn your thought to a belief.

Thoughts have no power but beliefs have the power of the faith that you have.

Thoughts are not enough for creating emotions. There are some thoughts that pass through your mind and there are instances when you find these thoughts funny. Later on, when you try to look at things from a different viewpoint, you feel different regarding an exactly same thing. Your most embarrassing moment when you were in high school might have been the worst nightmare of your life that week. But with a bigger perspective of time, say, 30 years after, it will just become nothing but a mere source of genuine laughter. Even after 30 years, the history of that event is still the same but over time, your perspective has already changed and together with this, your emotions also change.

The quality of your emotion in terms of pain or pleasure that you make will largely depend on how you look at things or your point of view. The emotions' intensity that you create during that moment will depend on the amount of fait that you invested in the assumptions and beliefs that support that thought. Faith in some beliefs is the power source behind every emotion that you have. Get your faith from all the beliefs that surround a thought and you will surely be able to alter the emotions that you feel.

The emotions that stem from your thoughts are the product of your point of view, your underlying beliefs and the amount of power that you put in them in the form of faith. In case you are trying to alter your emotional state through altering just your thoughts, you will never be able to succeed.

Attempting to alter your emotions without changing your viewpoint, faith investment and underlying assumptions will probably fail. It will be like building a chair with a single leg and expecting this to give you the support that you need.

If you want to change your emotional reactions, emotional state and put more happiness into your life, it is a must that you change your point of view and recover your faith from the false beliefs that you have.

CHAPTER 4

NOTE YOUR SURROUNDINGS
AND CIRCUMSTANCES

Synopsis

When you are emotional, there are other things that you have to consider, and these will include your surroundings and circumstances. By taking these things into account, it will be much easier for you to balance your emotions not only based on what you feel but also based on those around you.

Your Emotions and the Environment

When you are surrounded by noise, clutter and chaos, it is only natural for you to feel irritable and stressed all day. In the end, it is definitely hard to find some moments for self reflection and self awareness when your surroundings and the circumstances around you is not conducive to Zen and relaxation. In the same way, it can be hard to cope with your problems when all that you see around are people that rush here and there, vehicles that speed away at a neck breaking speed, and a dizzy whirl of commerce that goes nonstop. You will surely wish that you have the power to slow things down just so you can feel much lighter.

When taking note of your surroundings and circumstances, it is a must for you to understand how your environment can affect your emotions. Your are surrounded by tons of stressors and if you will not take extra care, you might unnecessarily end up exposing yourself to the risk factors that can lead to mental health problems, something that you will surely not want to happen in your case. It is also advisable that you include management of your surroundings as a part of your agenda when taking care of your emotional wellbeing.

So, how will you create a good environment that can help improve your emotions?

Mood and Colors

There is a scientific explanation to the effect of color on the mood or emotion of a person. Various colors emit various light frequencies and these can all affect the emotions of people in different ways. If you like to de- stress, it is best to expose yourself to plenty of blue as this is known for helping in decreasing the blood pressure of a person. Meanwhile, yellows can inspire happiness so ensure that your surrounding has spatters of yellow. But, stay away from reds for these are known for triggering aggression and anger and even hypertension.

Spaces of Green are a Must

Humans need contact with nature. It has been found out that seeing life around you can give you a relaxing feeling and it also provides chemicals required for zeroing out stress that you can get through exposure to trees, plants and animals. Make sure that you take a regular stroll in the park or put some potted plants by your desk or window. Mother Nature offers free and accessible ways for making your emotions better and it is a must to make the most out of them.

Privacy Also Matters

A certain study discovered that an open lay out in offices are not conducive to the productivity and focus of workers. Cubicles are needed for privacy for you not to get distracted by what other people in front of, behind, or beside you are doing.

The insecure feeling that comes from the feeling that someone is constantly watching you can be the cause of stress. If you are working, ask for some privacy not to be uppity but to take care of your emotional health.

Take Note of Weather Changes

Climate change is becoming more evident than ever and based on research, the rapid changes in weather conditions can have an effect on your emotions. For example, heat waves have become longer, stronger and more often than what they used to and the onset of these can have an impact people who are already emotional. Anxiety and stress can also happen when there is an impending disastrous weather condition, particularly for those that leave near the vulnerable areas. Knowing how changes in the climate can result to emotional problems is the initial step to prevent the start or worsening of emotional concerns.

CHAPTER 5

BRAINSTORM OTHER RESPONSES

Synopsis

There are instances when you do not know how to react or respond to a certain situation. Should you be angry? Should you resent? Should you be happy or satisfied? When facing a difficult situation, it is important that you brainstorm the different responses that are available for you in order to handle things properly.

Choose Your Emotional Response to Situations

Conflicts will always be a part of your life. At times, these conflicts take place just when you least expect them. But remember that all conflicts can always be resolved when handled and dealt with properly.

The process of conflict resolution should actually start with controlling your emotional response. Some people might say that they react that way because they can't help but the truth is, self control is more than possible.

During difficult situations, you and you alone have the power to choose your responses. There might be occasions when you will lose control. This is pretty much understandable but at the end of the day, you need to simply accept responsibility for your response before you work to keep yourself under complete emotional control from that specific point forward. You have to set the example that others can follow. Since the emotional system of humans takes majority of its input from the external sources, you might as well influence other people to control their emotional state at the same time. When brainstorming your responses, you must not only deal with your own response but also set the tone for others to follow as this can lead to a better environment around you.

CHAPTER 6

EVALUATE YOUR OPTIONS

Synopsis

As it so happens, your emotions are things that you create on your own but can be affected by other external factors. When you simply find it hard to rein in your feelings, it is best that you assess first the available options that are available before you react to a certain situation.

When things are not going your way, it is just too easy for you to be angry or irritated. If you have a lot of work to do and your internet connection is giving you a hard time, you will surely fire up and before you know it, your emotions have already taken over your system.

With the demands of today's fast paced life, it is just too common to see other people reacting impulsively to situations without really bothering to stop and evaluate things first. And when things are done on impulse, you can only expect that results will not be good and can even make the situation even worse.

Check Your Options Before You React

For instance, when the internet connection in your office is not working just when you have tons of deadline to finish on your desk, what should you do? Should you flare up and start throwing things? Will you shout and be the cause of commotion in the office? Will you just walk out of the office just like that?

Even though this kind of reactions are understandable especially when you have reached the critical level of your emotions, this do not really lessen your problem and instead, it will only further aggravate the issue which can soon backfire on no one else but you.

Instead of reacting, the best thing that you can do is sit down and start to evaluate the options that are available. You can call the internet provider directly or you can talk to your superior to see if you can at least do something about your deadlines and still be able to finish all your work for the day.

You see, things are really not as complicated as they are if you will be more rational and reduce being emotional. At the end of the day, there are plenty of options available and the only thing that you need to do is to stop, relax and clear your mind of your negative emotions. This way, the issue will be solved and you can get back on track without causing any serious damage to yourself and to those around you.

CHAPTER 7

DECIDE THE BEST ROUTE TO TAKE

Synopsis

If you want your emotions to be balanced, one of the things that you need to do is to decide on the perfect route that you need to take. Here, you have think wisely to and this chapter will give you some idea about it.

Many people tend to assume that emotions only happen to you and just like storms, the best that you can do is to just wait until these completely pass.

Change of Routes Helps Your Emotions However, unlike those climatic storms, you can actually influence or even alter your emotions with no need to resort to different unhealthy methods such as drugs or alcohol. Having the ability to influence or manage your emotions can be a powerful marker to achieve good health, an emotional maturity as well as overall happiness.

Instead of letting yourself be swallowed up in your emotions, the perfect thing that you can do is decide on the right route that you need to take. It means that you need to find some diversions. For instance, when you feel bored or flat, just sitting in front of the TV with its uninteresting show will only worsen things. Instead, switch this off and go for a walk around your neighborhood. A breath of fresh air can help a lot in inevitably changing your mood.

If you feel angry, you can focus on the three essential things in your life that you feel grateful. In case you are anxious, you can imagine that the thing that makes you anxious has already took place and has gone much better than what you expect.

Controlling your emotions is possible and it is even made easier when you are able to pinpoint the right route that you should take. All you need is to think or do something entirely different. Never be passively carried along by your present emotion and instead, let your mind work properly to steer you towards the right path.

CHAPTER 8

LEARN TO BE HAPPY WITH YOURSELF

Synopsis

The last but definitely not the least thing that you have to do in order to achieve optimum emotional balance is to learn how to be happy with yourself. Of course, your emotions will never be put in their right places when you yourself are not happy and satisfied in your own skin. In this last chapter, you will learn some easy ways on how to embrace happiness within yourself.

Did you ever find yourself standing in front of the mirror feeling hateful and resentful of yourself? Do you really understand how it is to be totally disgusted with yourself, feeling the longing for changes?

There are times when you feel upset about something and you allow the circumstances and environment to dictate whether you will be happy or not. But the stark truth is that if you live your life with happiness and choose what you will do all that it takes so that you can be happy, it is very possible for you to be happy when you put your mind to it.

Easy Steps Towards Your Own Happiness Happiness is something that you have to do on purpose. Even in the middle of difficulties and struggles, you have to choose to be happy. It is not something that comes from having things or money for the truth is, happiness stems from within you and you alone. Being happy with yourself simply means that you have to show mercy to yourself, forgive yourself, befriend yourself, accept yourself, and last but not the least, love yourself.

It is a lifetime journey that calls for regular self examination as well as a continuous process of making peace with yourself. It is all about discovering the things that make you unhappy and opting to live in true peace. This means that you treat yourself with kindness and compassion. This makes you start to enjoy your life even more, celebrating this to be a peaceful adventure. This helps you to live your life to the fullest, allowing you to make the whole world a much better place not only for you but also for others.

However, learning to be happy with yourself might be among the trickiest challenges that are going to face. For some people, such challenges can be too hard to handle, which is why they just let these rule their lives. There are also those who endure challenges but some choose to overcome them yet they do not have any idea how to do it.

If you want to be happy with yourself, here are some things that can help you out:

Self Forgiveness

You have to forgive yourself for having negative thoughts. Forgive yourself for not thinking twice and for talking. Forgive yourself for showing rudeness to your superior, parents, friends and siblings. Never think of negative thoughts about yourself for the wrong decisions or wrong steps. It is a type of thinking that will put your focus on the issue and not on the solution. It will be best that you say good things regarding yourself instead of saying negative things. Say positive things to yourself for it will be a sign that you already forgave yourself.

Don't Talk and Think about Your Issues

Try to focus instead on the good in all situations that you face and all persons that you have relationships with, which include yourself.

Forgive Other People

If you like to make peace with other people, forgive, forget and learn to let go of the things that happened in the past. Holding grudges and resenting is never good. To forgive easily, assume that they did no cause offense to you in the first place.

Be Busy

When you are busy, you will have less time to think particularly of someone or something that cause your negative feelings. Getting your hands full will keep the negative thoughts from triggering you over and over again.

Be a Blessing to Other People

Get your thoughts off yourself and instead, focus on being a blessing to those around you. Being a blessing to others results to more blessings coming back to you. This is an amazing phenomenon that not all people understand. Remember that life is not about receiving but more of giving.

Develop a Hobby

You can choose to spend your free time on listening to movies, reading, watching movies and other kinds of activities.

These will help take your mind off the issues in your life and thoughts that you have concerning yourself.

Accept Who You Are

Never focus on things about yourself which you cannot control. Never strive to become someone else. Never care about what other people say or think about you when you are not even sure if they are wrong or right. Once you do this, you will be able to free yourself of anxiety and stress. Accept who you are, be contented and hope to become a much better you.

Don't Lose Hope

Remember that even the darkest tunnels have a light at the end. Hope is the one thing that you can never afford to lose and with this, you can take the path towards your happiness. This reminds you that things will be alright.

With hope, you will be secured that whatever looks terrible is just a temporary occurrence and soon enough, things are going to turn out fine.

Be happy with yourself and soon enough, your emotions will be balanced out perfectly and success will be within easy reach.

Printed by Libri Plureos GmbH in Hamburg,
Germany